Sight Reading
SINGING
A progressive method
Initial–Grade 2

Ralph Allwood &
Andrew Morris

Published by
Trinity College London Press Ltd
trinitycollege.com

Registered in England
Company no. 09726123

Copyright © 2023 Trinity College London Press Ltd
First impression, March 2023

Unauthorised photocopying is illegal
No part of this publication may be copied or reproduced in any
form or by any means without the prior permission of the publisher.

Cover design by RF Design, rfportfolio.com
Printed in England by Halstan, Amersham, Bucks

Initial

Lesson 1

• **The interval of a major second**

A **major second** is the interval of a tone (or two semitones). Here is an example of a major second, which consists of two notes, C and D:

C   D

The examiner will play the first note (C) and ask you to repeat this followed by the second note (D).

1 Your teacher will play both C and D for you (the interval of a major second) and you should repeat this.

   Do this several times.

2 Your teacher will now play just the C for you and will ask you to sing both C and D.

Teacher   Your sung response

3 Do this several times.

Teacher   Your sung response

2

Initial

Think before you sing the interval:

Can you imagine the sound of the note D in your mind (once your teacher has given you a C)?

Yes ☐   No ☐

(This section applies to the exercises below.)

Accompanied Exercise

Your teacher will give you a C and accompany you singing C to D:

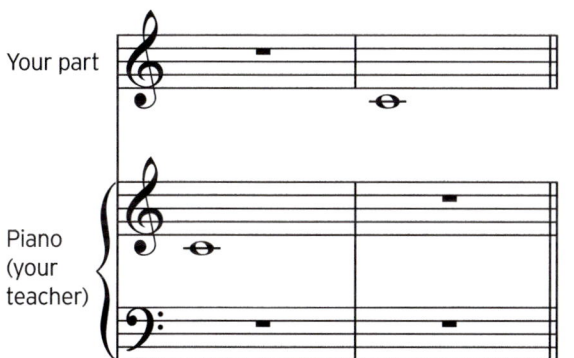

Your part

Piano (your teacher)

Your teacher will now just give you a C and ask you to sing C and then D:

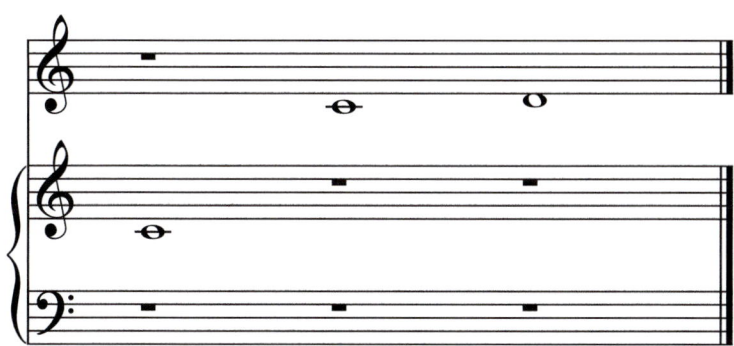

Do this several times.

Initial

Lesson 2

- **Practise reading the note value of a crotchet**

  ♩ A **crotchet** lasts for one beat.

  Bars create a division in music and are separated by vertical lines called bar lines.

You may notice that 2/4 has appeared at the start of each exercise below, this will be explained in lesson 3. Here are examples with two crotchets in a bar.

1 Clap this exercise.

2 Now say out loud the same notes to the letter 'C'.

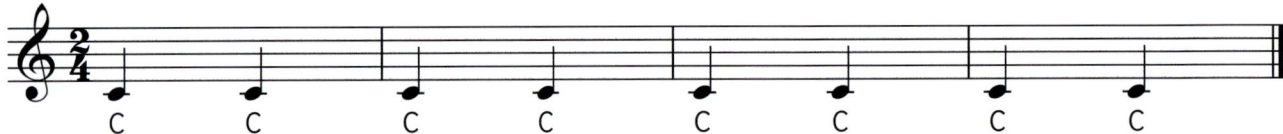

3 Your teacher will now sing or play a C and count two crotchet beats to show you the pulse. Sing the notes to the letter 'C' with your teacher.

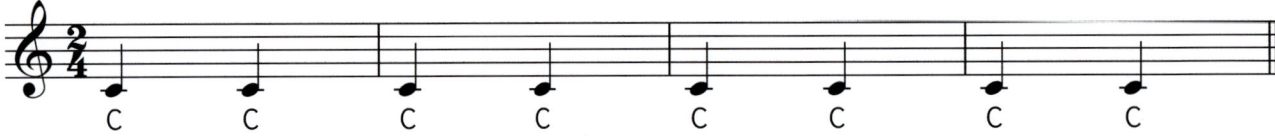

4 Now do this again on your own. Your teacher will remind you of the pitch and the pulse.

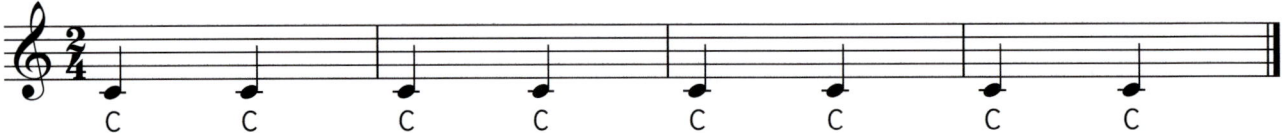

Initial

Think before you clap and sing:

Can you make all the crotchets even in rhythm and tone?   Yes ☐   No ☐

Accompanied Exercises

Your teacher will count two crotchet beats to show you the pulse before you clap or sing using the sound 'la', with your teacher playing the piano.

Your part

Piano (your teacher)

Sing to the letter 'C' after your teacher has given you the key chord and a C, and two bars of $\frac{2}{4}$ for the pulse.

Your part

Piano (your teacher)

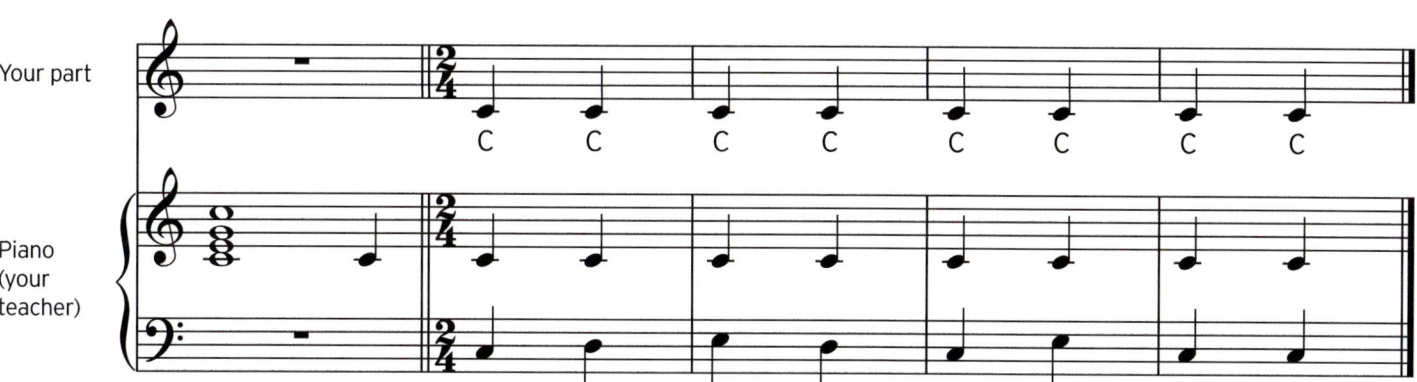

Initial

Lesson 3

- **Practise reading in the time signature 2/4**

2/4 means two crotchets in a bar. The 2 shows how many beats and the 4 indicates the kind of beat (crotchets).

1 Count two bars of 2/4 to set the pulse, then clap this exercise.

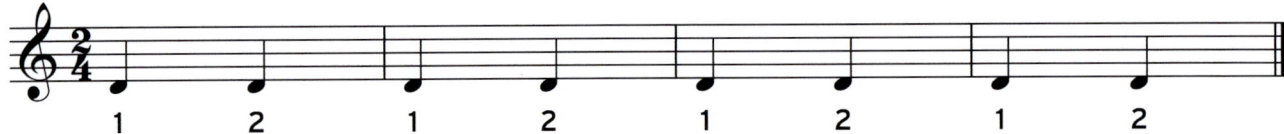

2 Now say out loud the names of the notes to the letter 'D'.

3 Your teacher will now give you the pitch of D and count you in two bars to show you the pulse. You sing the notes to the letter 'D' with your teacher.

4 Now do this again on your own. Your teacher will remind you of the pitch and the pulse.

6

Initial

Think before you clap and sing:

Do you know what $\frac{2}{4}$ means? Yes ☐ No ☐

Can you keep each note the same length? Yes ☐ No ☐

Accompanied Exercises

Your teacher will count in two bars of $\frac{2}{4}$ to show you the pulse before you clap or sing using the sound 'la', with your teacher playing the piano.

Sing to the letter D after your teacher has given you the key chord, first note and two bars of $\frac{2}{4}$ for the pulse.

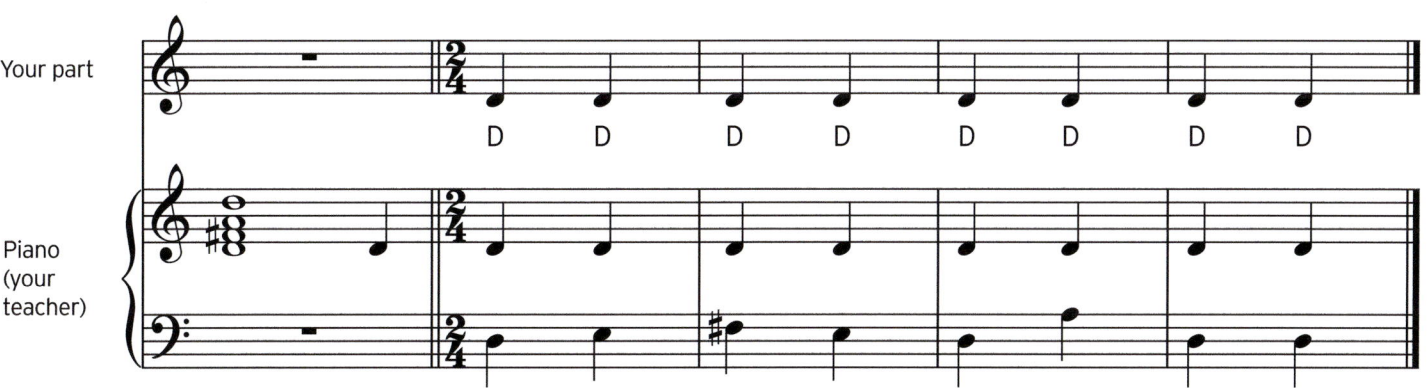

7

Initial

Lesson 4

- **Practise reading the pitches of C and D – an interval of a major second**

- **Practise recognising a pulse**

♩ = 72 means that there are 72 crotchets in a minute.

Sing these exercises to the word 'la'. The tempo (speed) for all these exercises is ♩ = 72.

1

2

3

4

5

Initial

Think before you sing:

Can you see the difference in the printed notes C and D?   Yes ☐   No ☐

Can you pitch the different sounds of C and D?   Yes ☐   No ☐

Do you understand what ♩ = 72 means?   Yes ☐   No ☐

Accompanied Exercises

Your teacher will play the key chord and the first note, and then count in two bars of 2/4 to give you the pulse before you start. Sing these exercises to the word 'la'.

Initial

Lesson 5

- **Practise singing the note E as well as the notes C and D in ascending phrases**

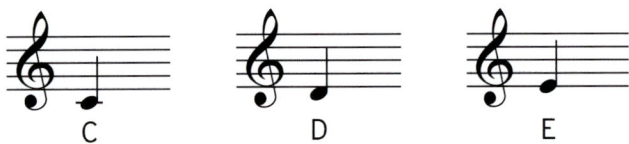

C   D   E

- **Learn to sing the E in tune**

Sing these exercises to the word 'la'.

1

2

3

4

5

Initial

Think before you sing:

Can you read the note E easily?   Yes ☐   No ☐

Can you sing the note E in tune? Yes ☐   No ☐

Accompanied Exercises

Your teacher will play the key chord and the first note, and then count in two bars of 2/4 to give you the pulse before you start. Sing these exercises to the word 'la'.

11

Initial

Lesson 6

- Practise singing the note E as well as the notes C and D both ascending and descending

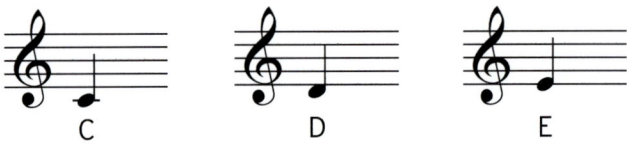

Notice the *mf* sign. This is an abbreviation of *mezzo-forte*. *Forte* means 'loud' and *mezzo* means 'half' or 'fairly', so we interpret *mf* as being moderately loud.

Sing these exercises to the word 'la'.

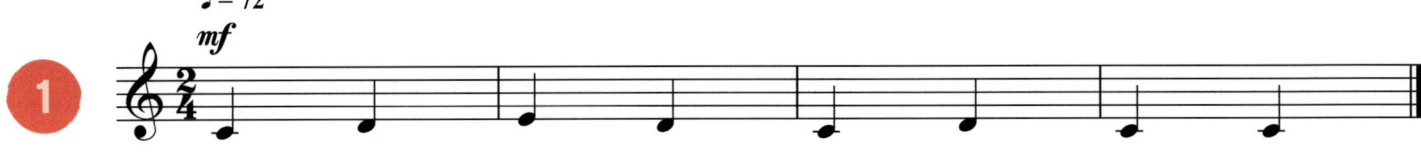

Initial

Think before you sing:

Can you still read the note E easily?   Yes ☐   No ☐

Can you sing all three notes, C, D and E, comfortably?   Yes ☐   No ☐

Accompanied Exercises

Your teacher will play the key chord and the first note, and then count in two bars of 2/4 to give you the pulse before you start. Sing these exercises to the word 'la'.

13

Initial

Lesson 7

- Practise reading repeated notes (which can often catch you out!)
- Learn to spot repeated notes in a melody

Circle all the repeated notes in the exercises below, then sing these exercises to the word 'la'.

1

2

3

4

5

Initial

Think before you sing:

Can you sing repeated notes correctly? Yes ☐ No ☐

Can you spot some repeated notes in the exercises below? Yes ☐ No ☐

Accompanied Exercises

Your teacher will play the key chord and the first note, and then count in two bars of 2/4 to give you the pulse before you start. Sing these exercises to the word 'la'.

Initial

Lesson 8

- Practise spotting musical patterns

Draw a box around bars which contain the same notes. Draw a circle around notes that are repeated, then sing these exercises to the word 'la'.

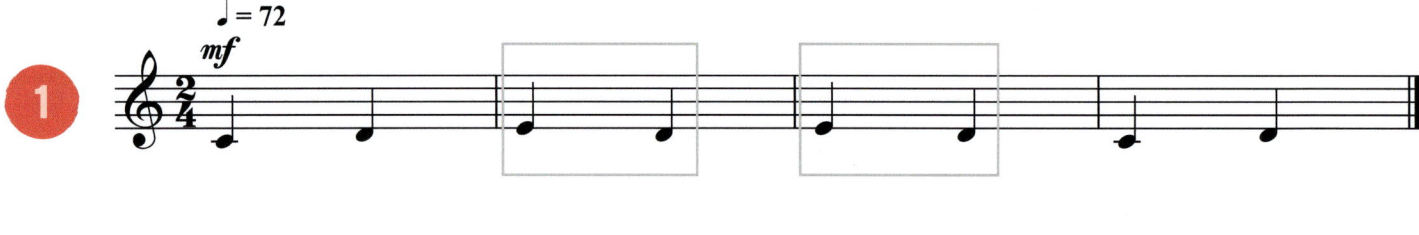

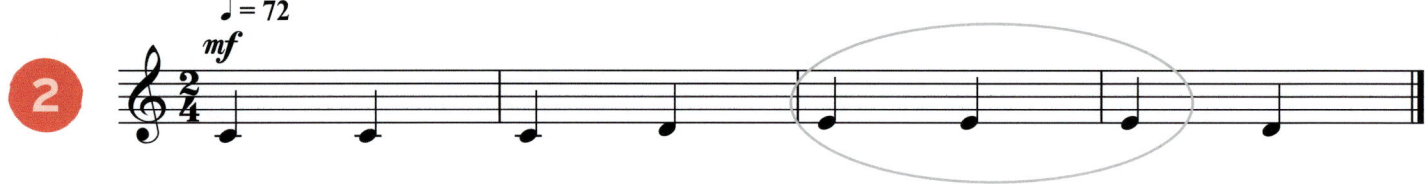

Initial

Think before you sing:

Can you recognise some musical patterns in the exercises below?   Yes ☐   No ☐

Can you sing musical patterns with confidence?   Yes ☐   No ☐

Accompanied Exercises

Your teacher will play the key chord and the first note, and then count in two bars of 2/4 to give you the pulse before you start. Sing these exercises to the word 'la'.

Initial

Lesson 9

- **Practise singing the beginning part of a major scale**
- Learn to sing each note in tune (especially the third – the E)

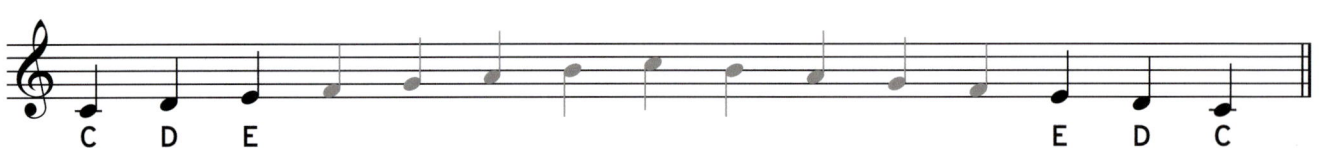
C D E   E D C

Sing these exercises to the word 'la'.

1

2

3

4

5

Initial

Think before you sing:

Can you spot the first three notes of a major scale? Yes ☐ No ☐

Can you pitch each note in tune? Yes ☐ No ☐

Accompanied Exercises

Your teacher will play the key chord and the first note, and then count in two bars of 2/4 to give you the pulse before you start. Sing these exercises to the word 'la'.

19

Initial

Lesson 10

- Practise putting together all that you have learnt so far
- Learn to sing these phrases with an even tone throughout

Sing these exercises to the word 'la'.

1

2

3

4

5

Initial

Think before you sing:

Can you read all the notes and sing them accurately?   Yes ☐   No ☐

Can you sing each phrase with an even tone?   Yes ☐   No ☐

Accompanied Exercises

Your teacher will play the key chord and the first note, and then count in two bars of 2/4 to give you the pulse before you start. Sing these exercises to the word 'la'.

Initial

Specimen Sight Reading Tests

Remember to use all of the ideas and techniques from the previous lessons when approaching sight reading.

1a. Interval Test
Please sing this note, and a major second above it. **[Play the lower note of the two printed]**

1b. Rhythm Test
Please clap the rhythm of this line straight through. **[Clap the pulse while counting 2 bars aloud]**

1c. Sung Test
You have 30 seconds to prepare for the sung part of the test, during which time you may practise aloud. You can choose which sound you use for this part of the test (dee/da/la).
[Play the key chord and starting note before and after the 30 seconds. Count 2 bars aloud.]

2a. Interval Test

2b. Rhythm Test

2c. Sung Test

3a. Interval Test

3b. Rhythm Test

3c. Sung Test

Initial

4a. Interval Test

4b. Rhythm Test

4c. Sung Test

5a. Interval Test

5b. Rhythm Test

5c. Sung Test

6a. Interval Test

6b. Rhythm Test

6c. Sung Test

7a. Interval Test

7b. Rhythm Test

7c. Sung Test

Initial

8a. Interval Test

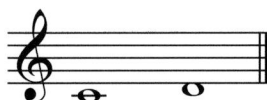

8b. Rhythm Test

8c. Sung Test

9a. Interval Test

9b. Rhythm Test

9c. Sung Test

10a. Interval Test

10b. Rhythm Test

10c. Sung Test

Grade 1

Lesson 1

- **Practise reading the note values crotchet and minim**

  ♩ **minim.** A minim lasts for two crotchet beats.

Clap the rhythms below whilst saying the pulse out loud '1, 2'. Then sing the pitches to the note letter names.

1
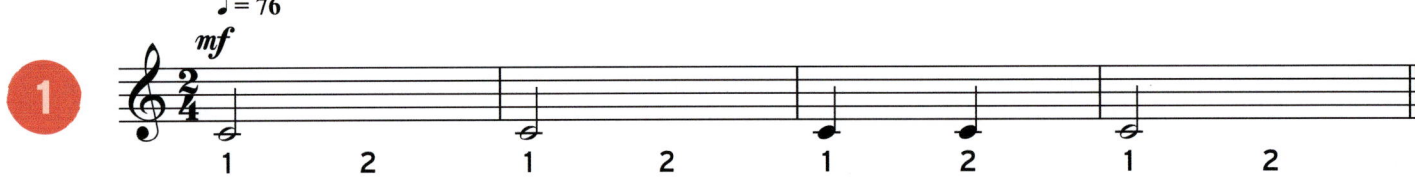

2
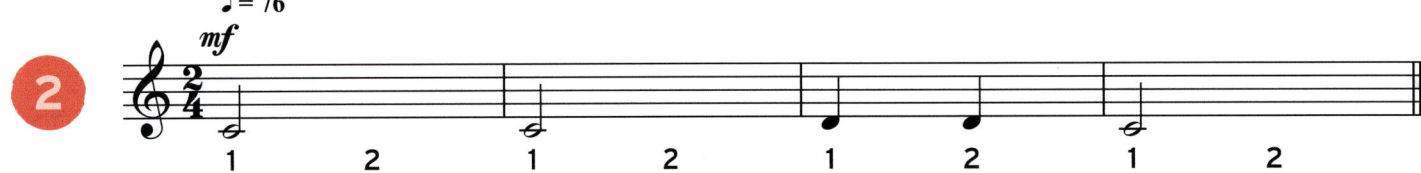

3
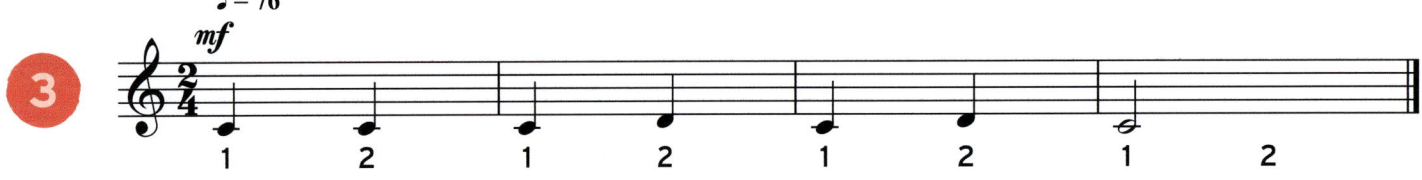

4
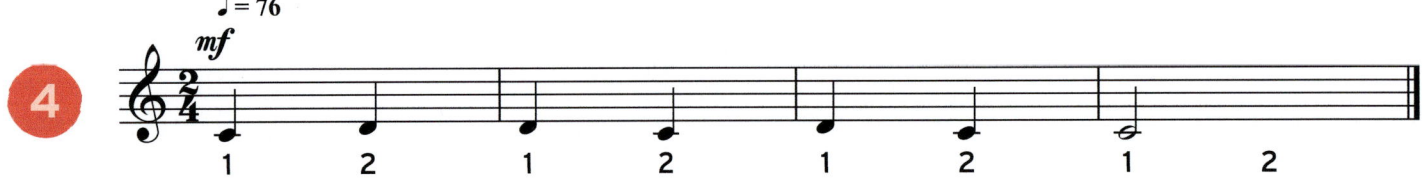

5
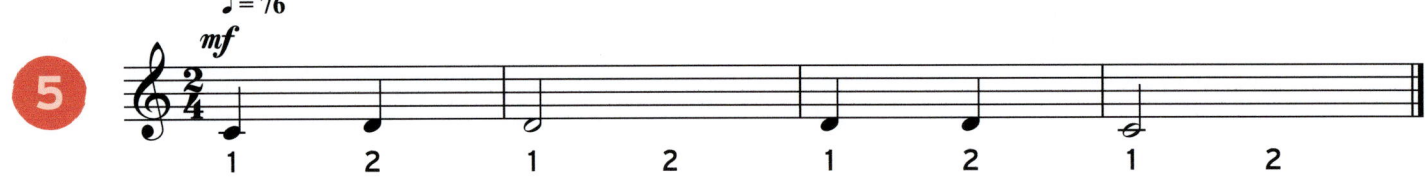

28

Grade 1

Think before you sing:

Can you hear the starting note and sing a major second above it   Yes ☐   No ☐

Do you know the difference between a crotchet and a minim?   Yes ☐   No ☐

Accompanied Exercise

You will be given a key chord and the starting note. Take some time to hear the two notes of the test in your mind and check the rhythm.

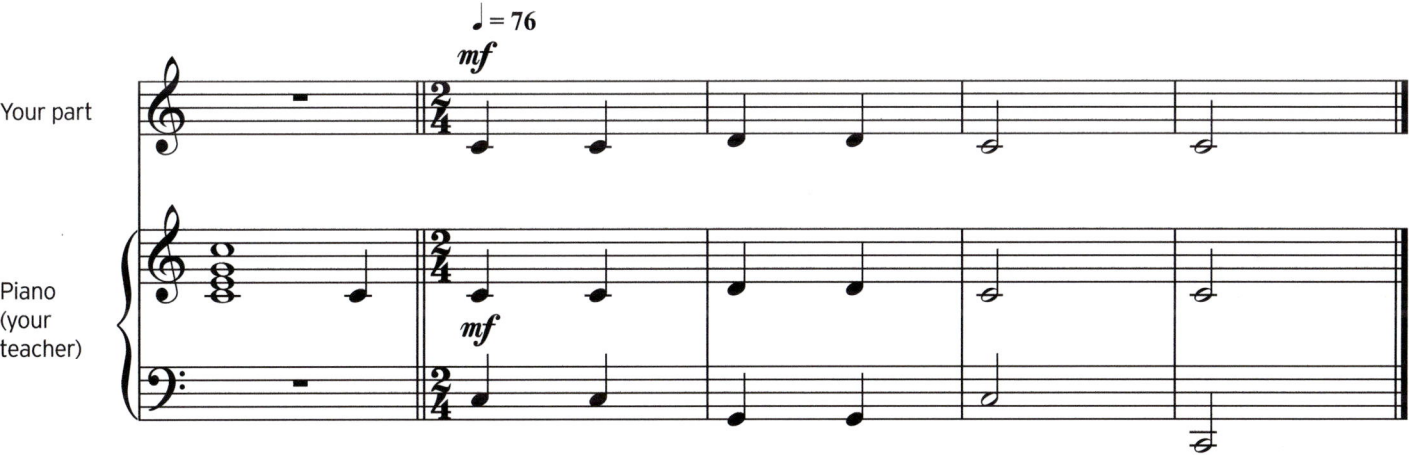

Grade 1

Lesson 2

- Additional practise with minims

First, say these rhythms to the syllable 'la' on one pitch whilst clapping the pulse.

Then find a middle C from a keyboard, instrument or app on your phone and sing the exercises to the note names C, D or E.

Try to read ahead – when you do this, you take in and process more information.

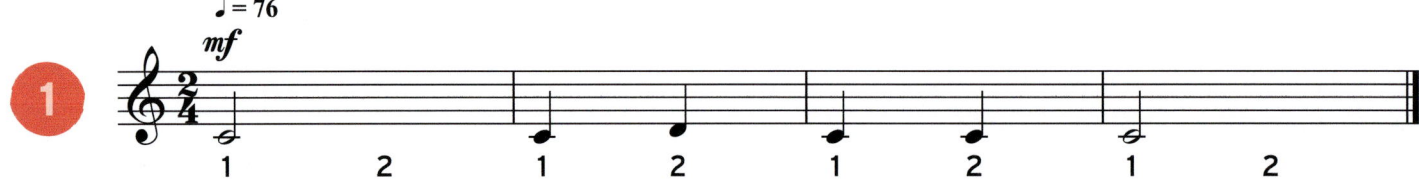

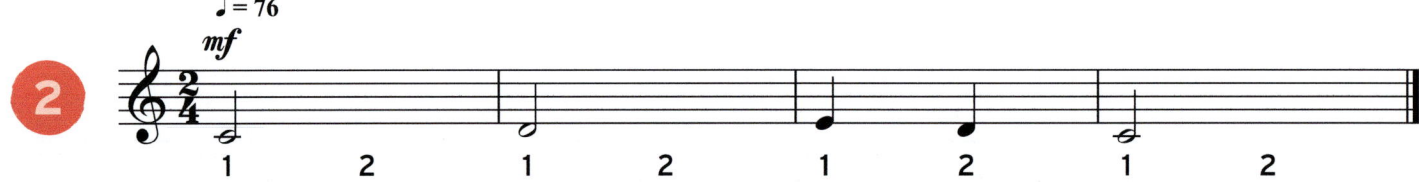

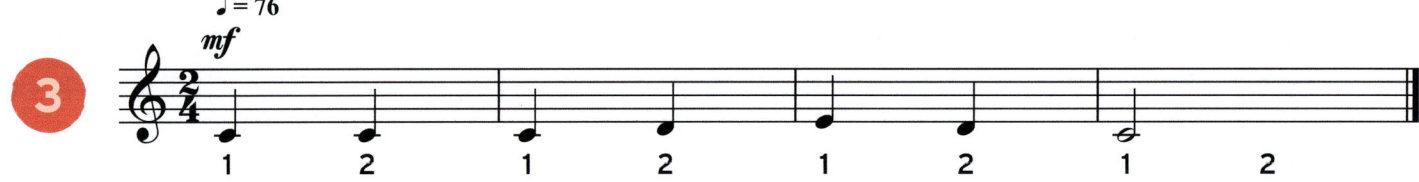

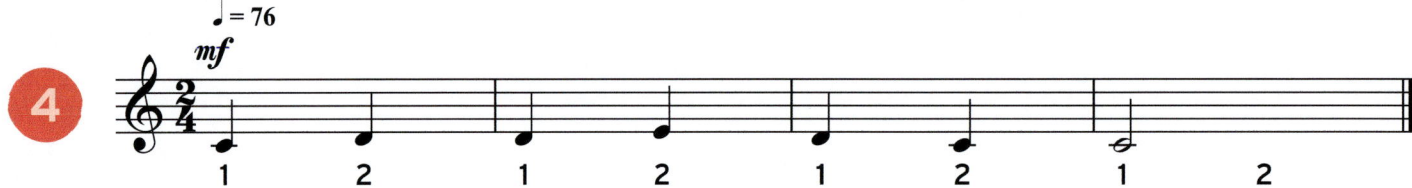

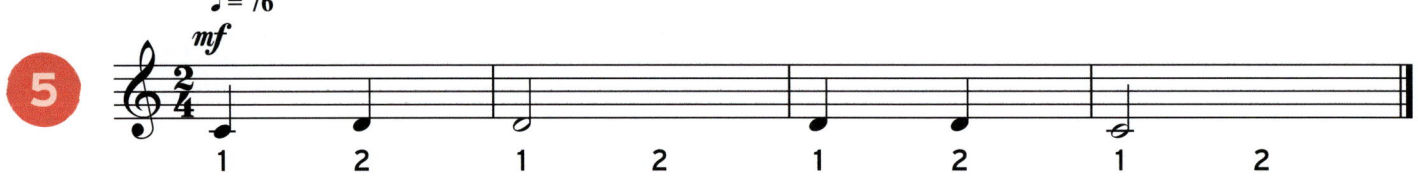

Grade 1

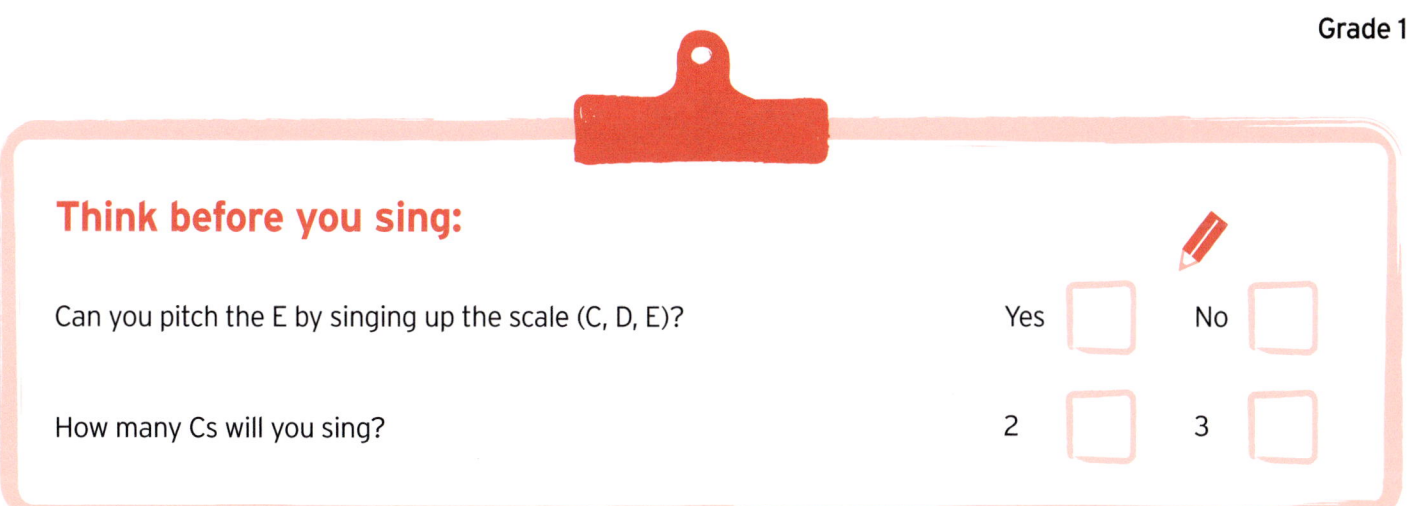

Think before you sing:

Can you pitch the E by singing up the scale (C, D, E)?   Yes ☐   No ☐

How many Cs will you sing?   2 ☐   3 ☐

Accompanied Exercise

Your teacher will play the key chord and your first note. Work out an E by singing up the scale from C.
Tap the rhythm first and make sure you can hear that E before you start.

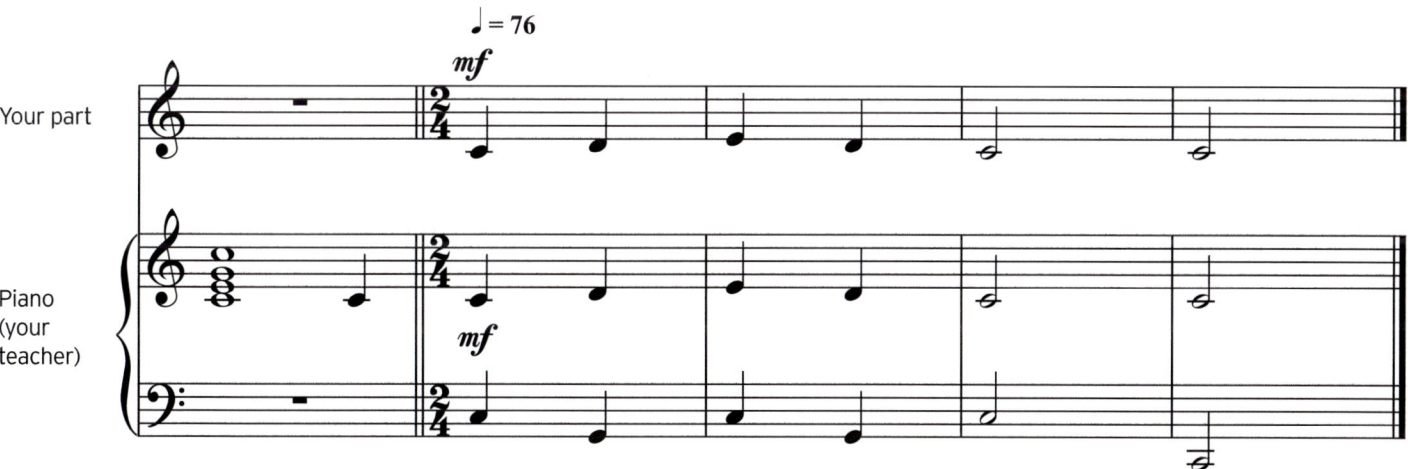

Lesson 3

- Additional exercises using the major second and minims

First say these rhythms to the syllable 'la'. Then find a C from a keyboard, instrument or app on your phone. Then sing these exercises using the note names C, D, E.

Notice the difference between the third bars of the first two exercises. Count 1, 2 for each bar. That will eventually become automatic.

Grade 1

Think before you sing:

Can you pitch the first three notes of the major scale correctly?   Yes ☐   No ☐

A minim lasts for two beats   Yes ☐   No ☐

Accompanied Exercise

Work out a C, D and an E from the key chord before you start.

Grade 1

Lesson 4

- **The interval of a minor third**
- **Introducing the note F**

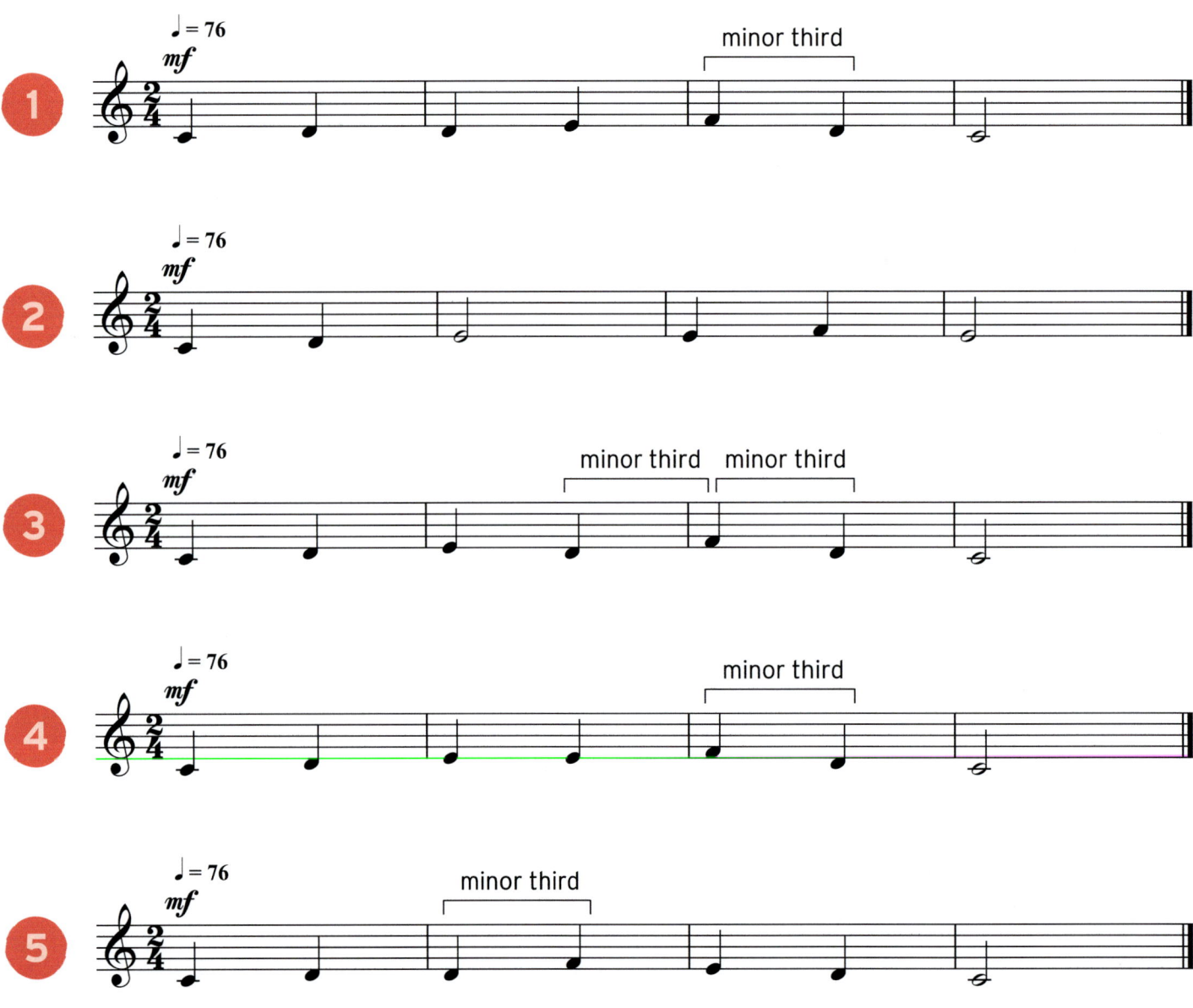

In this lesson we extend the notes up to F.

If you find these exercises easy, still do them, because it will make you more able to do the more complex ones later on.

First say the rhythms to the syllable 'la'. Then find a C from a keyboard, instrument or app on your phone. Then sing these exercises to the note names of C, D, E, F.

Grade 1

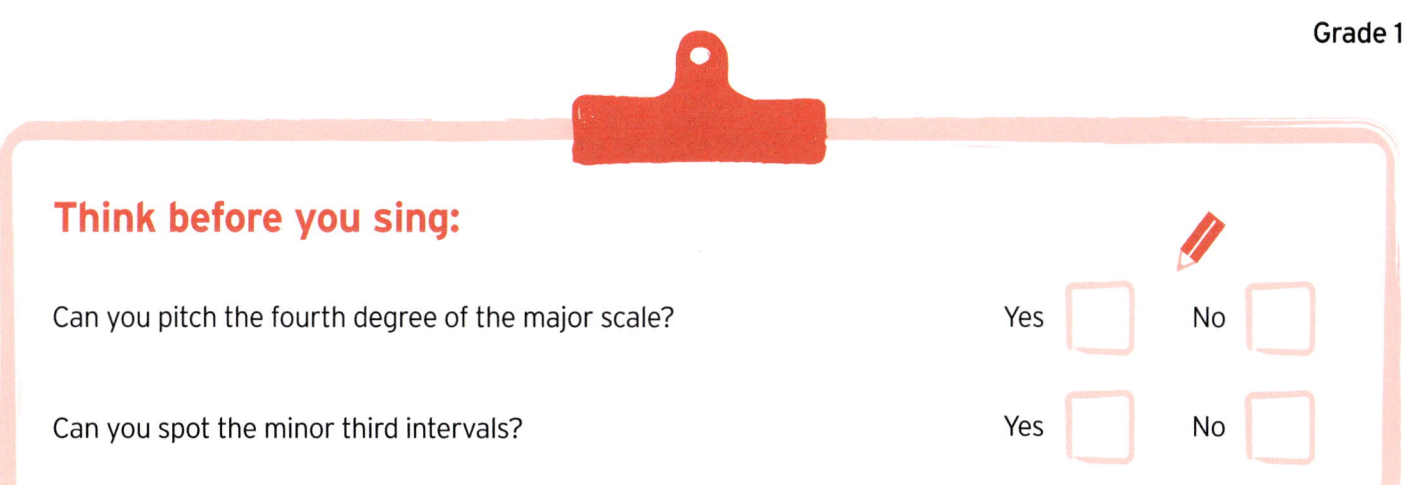

Think before you sing:

Can you pitch the fourth degree of the major scale? Yes ☐ No ☐

Can you spot the minor third intervals? Yes ☐ No ☐

Accompanied Exercise

Remember the C you sing at the beginning: it will be useful for the last note, even if you have sung the F wrong!

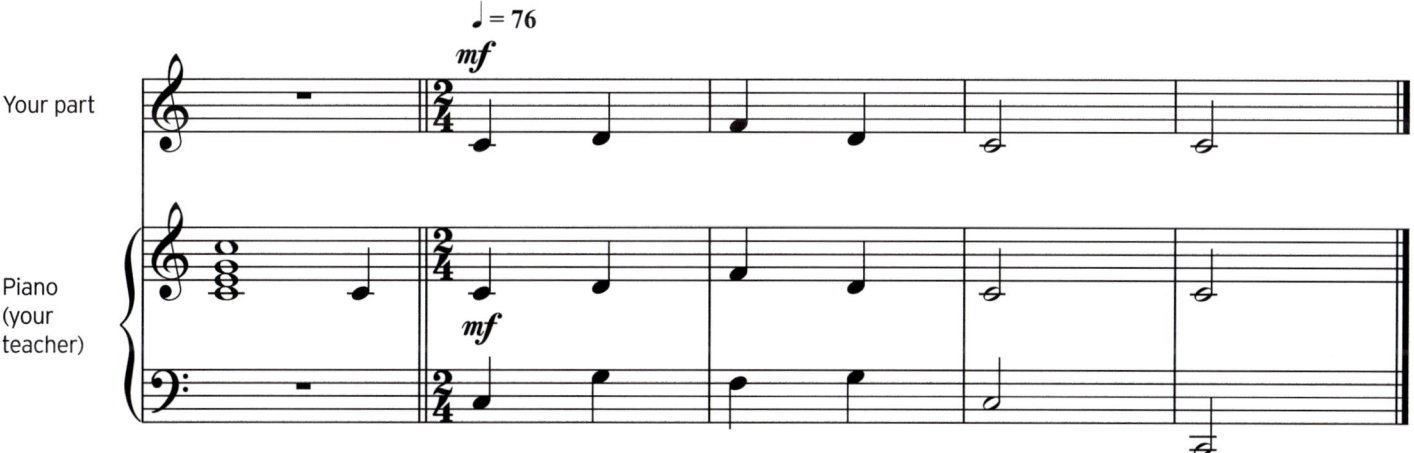

35

Grade 1

Lesson 5

- Finding the thirds

Do these exercises, even if you find them easy. They will help you to do the more complex ones later on.

The minor third interval occurs at least once in each of the exercises below. See if you can find them all and mark each with a circle.

After you've found all the thirds, say the rhythms to the syllable 'la'.

Then find a C from a keyboard, instrument or app on your phone. Then sing these exercises to C, D, E, F.

Grade 1

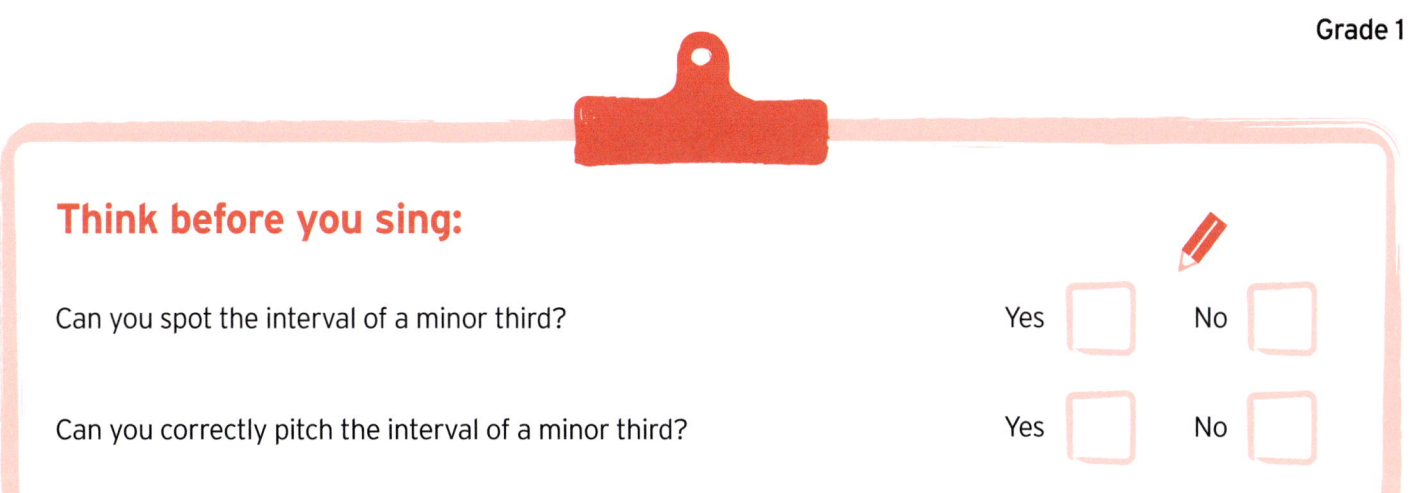

Think before you sing:

Can you spot the interval of a minor third? Yes ☐ No ☐

Can you correctly pitch the interval of a minor third? Yes ☐ No ☐

Accompanied Exercise

Look at the whole four-bar passage and you will see that the awkwardness is at the end.

Remember the C you sing at the beginning: it will be useful for the last note.

Grade 1

Lesson 6

- More work on minor thirds

In this lesson we continue practising the minor third. Spot each of the minor thirds before you begin, and get used to the sound of this interval.

38

Grade 1

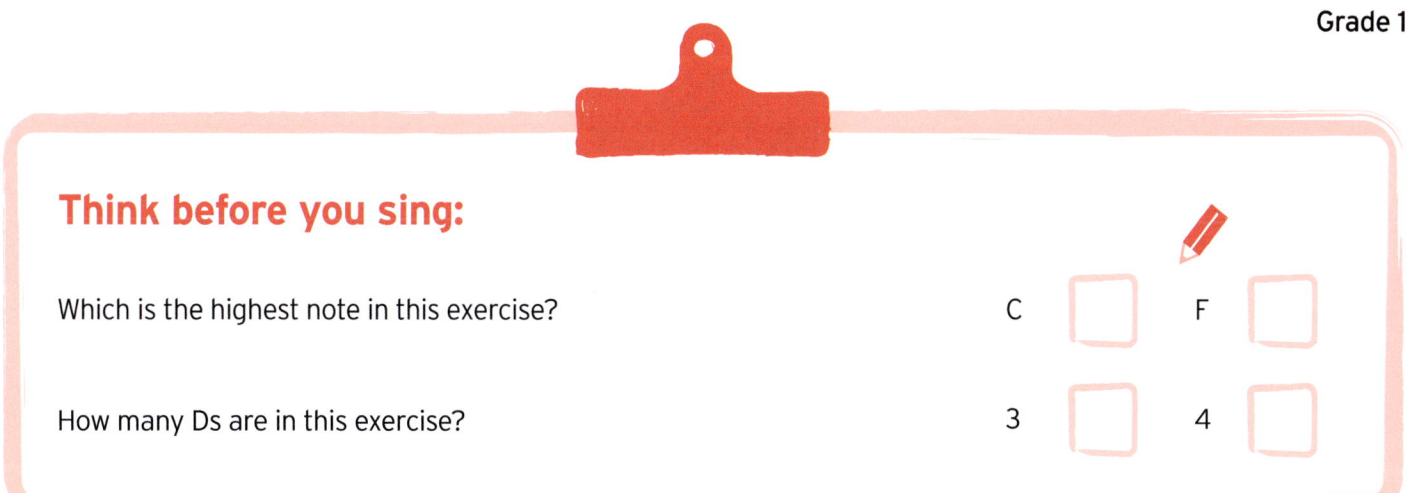

Think before you sing:

Which is the highest note in this exercise? C ☐ F ☐

How many Ds are in this exercise? 3 ☐ 4 ☐

Accompanied Exercise

Begin by spotting where the minor third occurs and see if you can imagine the interval in your mind.

Grade 1

Lesson 7

- Another minor third within C-G
- Introducing the note G

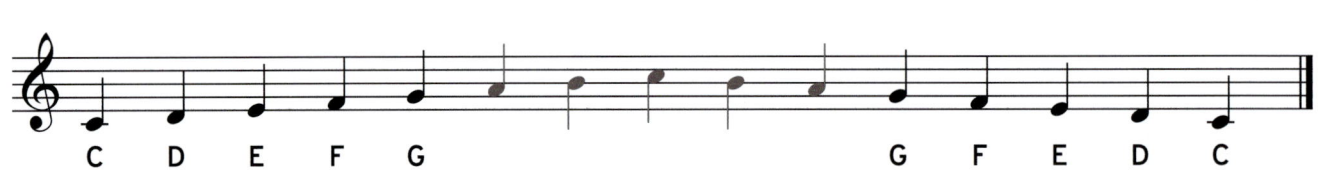

If you find these exercises easy, still do them, because it will make you more able to do the more complex ones later on. We are learning most when we get things right. If you find them hard, do them several times.

The minor third we used in the previous lesson occurs several times in the exercises below. Can you spot them? There is also another minor third. Can you spot that? It is between the notes E and G (if you are going up), or G and E (if you are coming down).

It may help you to correctly sing the intervals by remembering the pitch of certain notes as you sing. For example, the dotted lines show the note you could hold in your memory until you come across it again to make the interval.

Once you have found all the minor thirds, sing these exercises to their note names.

1
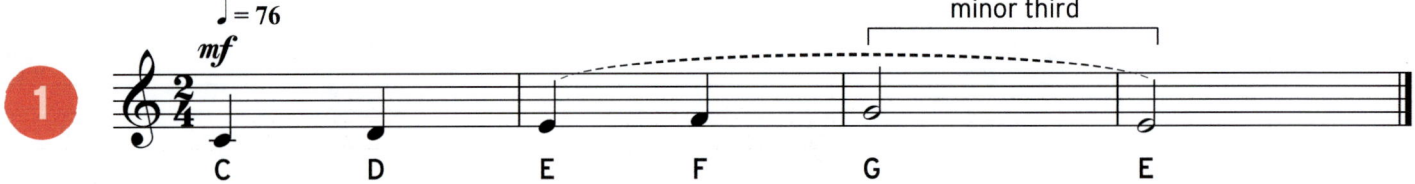

2

3

4
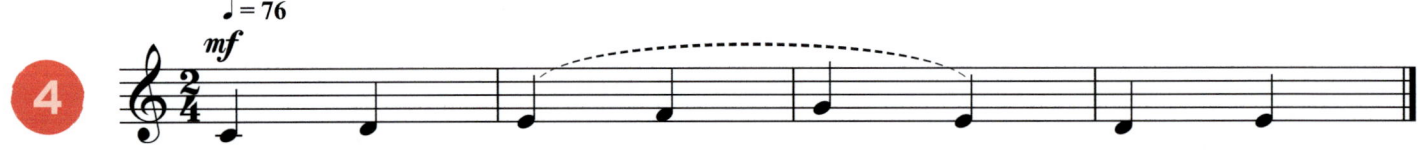

5
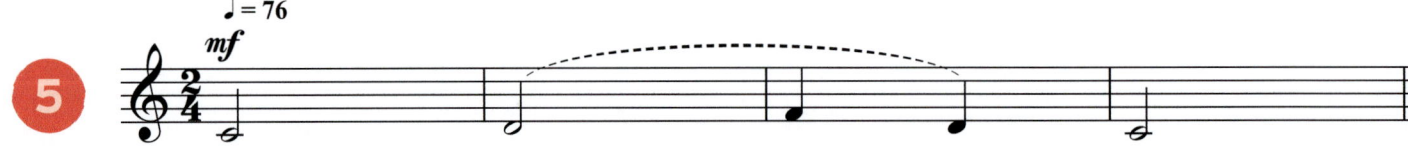

Grade 1

Think before you sing:

Sing the notes C, D, E, F, G before you begin the exercise below.

Be particularly careful of the D. Be aware that it is right next to the C.

Hear the melody in your head before you begin.

Accompanied Exercise

Grade 1

Lesson 8

- Mixed thirds

In this lesson we add a few little challenges within the range of a fifth.

First say the rhythms to the syllable 'la'.

Then sing the exercises to C, D, E, F, G.

Draw dotted lines on the exercises below to help you remember pitches from earlier in the exercise.

1
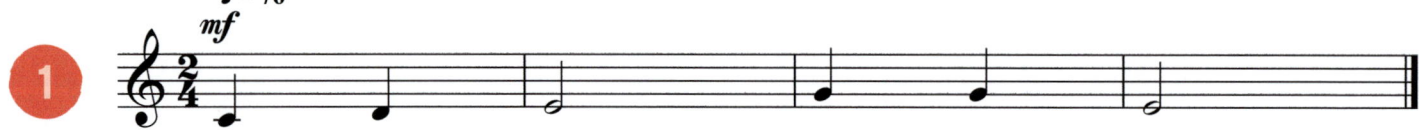

2
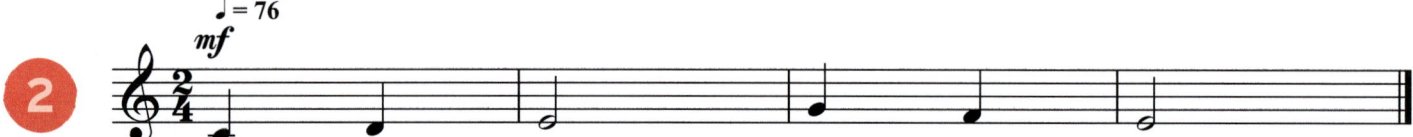

3

4

5

Grade 1

Think before you sing:

Sing the notes C, D, E, F, G before you begin the exercise below

Hear the melody in your head before you begin.

Accompanied Exercise

Grade 1

Lesson 9

- Spotting patterns

In this lesson we add a few more challenges within the range of a fifth.

Sing the exercises to C, D, E, F, G. You will see that these note names are not given.

The first exercise has three melodic ideas marked. Go through the remaining exercises marking where the same pitches appear. They may have different rhythms and may also start halfway through the bar!

Grade 1

Think before you sing:

Sing the notes C, D, E, F, G before you begin the exercise below

Hear the melody in your head before you begin

Bracket the minor third

Accompanied Exercise

Grade 1

Lesson 10

- More patterns to spot

Draw a circle and line between notes that are the same in the following exercises. Then sing them to their note names.

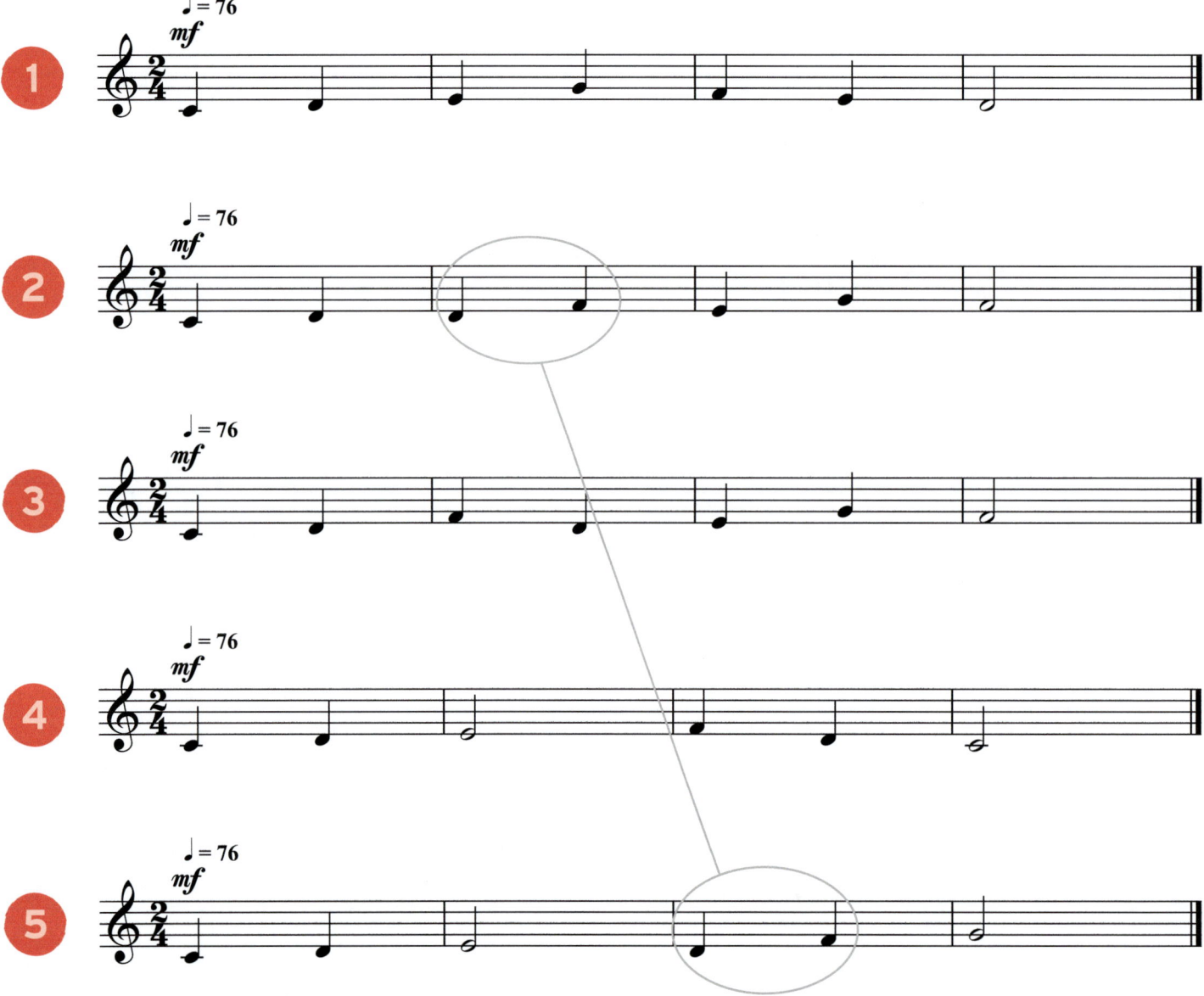

Grade 1

Think before you sing:

Sing the notes C, D, E, F, G before you begin the exercise below

Hear the melody in your head before you begin.

Can you spot the minor thirds?

Accompanied Exercise

Grade 1

Specimen Sight Reading Tests

Remember to use all of the ideas and techniques from the previous lessons when approaching sight reading.

1a. Interval Test
Please sing this note, and a minor third above it. **[Play the lower note of the two printed]**

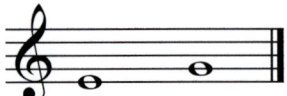

1b. Rhythm Test
Please clap the rhythm of this line straight through. **[Clap the pulse while counting 2 bars aloud]**

1c. Sung Test
You have 30 seconds to prepare for the sung part of the test, during which time you may practise aloud. You can choose which sound you use for this part of the test (dee/da/la).
[Play the key chord and starting note before and after the 30 seconds. Count 2 bars aloud.]

2a. Interval Test

2b. Rhythm Test

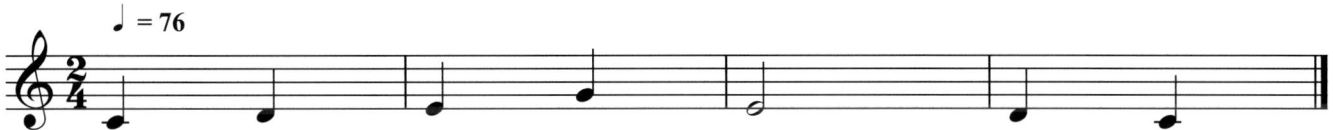

2c. Sung Test

3a. Interval Test

3b. Rhythm Test

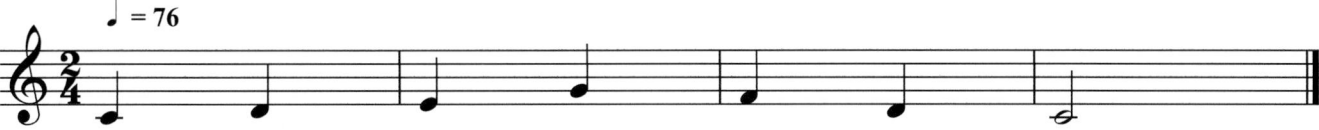

3c. Sung Test

Grade 1

4a. Interval Test

4b. Rhythm Test

4c. Sung Test

5a. Interval Test

5b. Rhythm Test

5c. Sung Test

Grade 1

6a. Interval Test

6b. Rhythm Test

6c. Sung Test

7a. Interval Test

7b. Rhythm Test

7c. Sung Test

Grade 1

8a. Interval Test

8b. Rhythm Test

8c. Sung Test

9a. Interval Test

9b. Rhythm Test

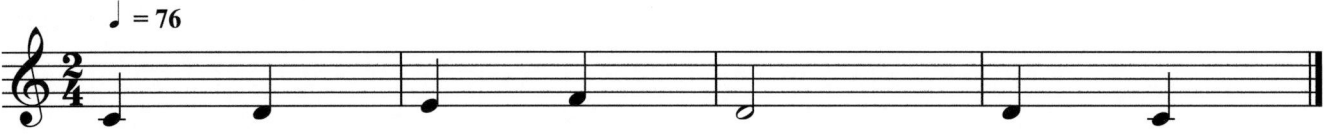

9c. Sung Test

10a. Interval Test

10b. Rhythm Test

10c. Sung Test

Grade 2

Lesson 1

- **Practise reading in the time signature 3/4**

- 3/4 means three crotchets in a bar. The 3 shows how many beats and the 4 indicates the kind of beat (crotchets).

- 𝅗𝅥. **dotted minim.** A dotted minim lasts for three crotchet beats

Tap the rhythm first, then hum the tonic (key note) and go from there.

Take your time. If there is an awkward interval, slow down and work it out. In an exam you have to keep going, ideally, but in exercises you will learn more if you take your time to work it out rather than guessing it.

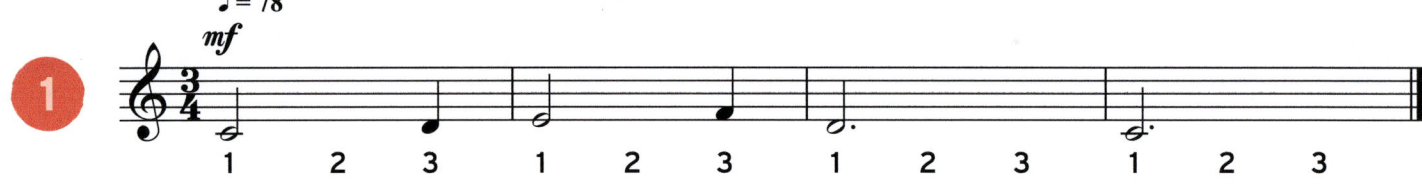

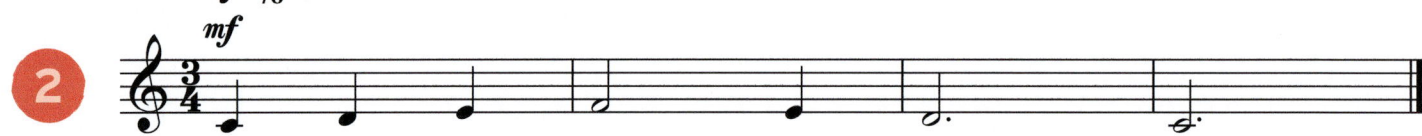

Grade 2

Think before you sing:

Start by checking which time signature you are in - is it $\frac{2}{4}$ or $\frac{3}{4}$?

Check the note values

Look for tricky intervals

Accompanied Exercise

Grade 2

Lesson 2

- **The key of F major**

Pieces in the key of F major usually use B flats all the way through. To keep things simple, composers use a key signature at the beginning of every stave to show the singer that all the Bs in the piece (whatever the register) are lowered to B flat.

Tap the rhythm first, then hum the tonic (key note) and go from there.

Take your time. If there is an awkward interval, slow down and work it out.

Grade 2

Think before you sing:

Start by checking which time signature you are in – is it $\frac{2}{4}$ or $\frac{3}{4}$?

Next, check the key signature – is the key C major or F major?

Identify your starting note, and acknowledge the tricky parts of the phrase.

Accompanied Exercise

Lesson 3

- **The key of G major**

Pieces in the key of G major usually use F sharps all the way through. The key signature shows that all the Fs in the piece (whatever the register) are raised to F sharp.

- **The major third**

In the key of G major you will find a major third between the notes G and B.

You will notice that there aren't any F sharps for you to sing in these exercises, but the new key signature also tells us what key we are singing in. This is the key of G major, so the tonic (or root note) is G. Also notice that there are minor thirds in these exercises too – between A and C, and B and D.

58

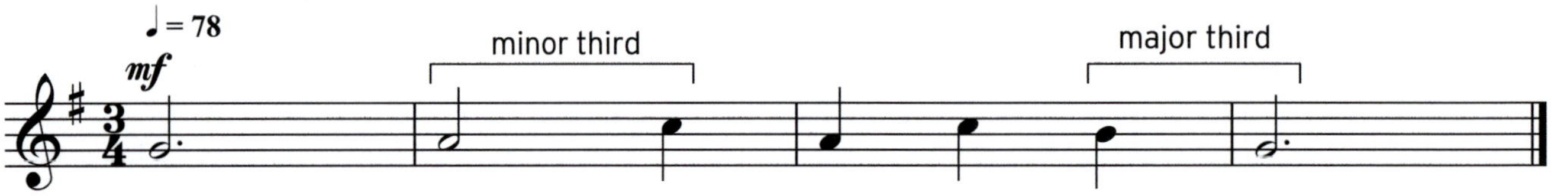

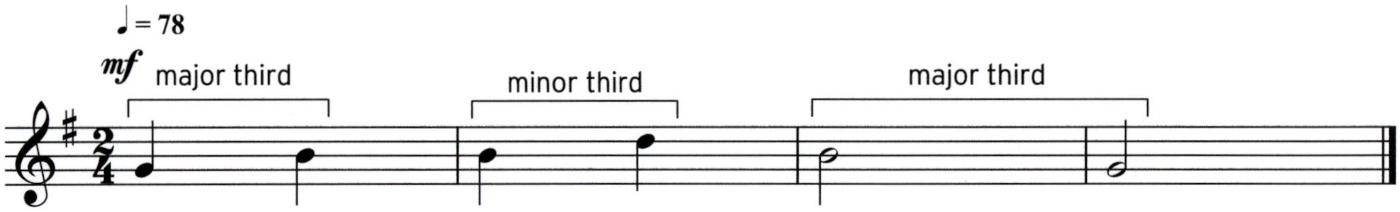

Grade 2

Think before you sing:

Can you work out which key the exercise is in – F or G major?

Can you recognise the interval of a major third?

Can you pitch the interval of a major third?

Accompanied Exercise

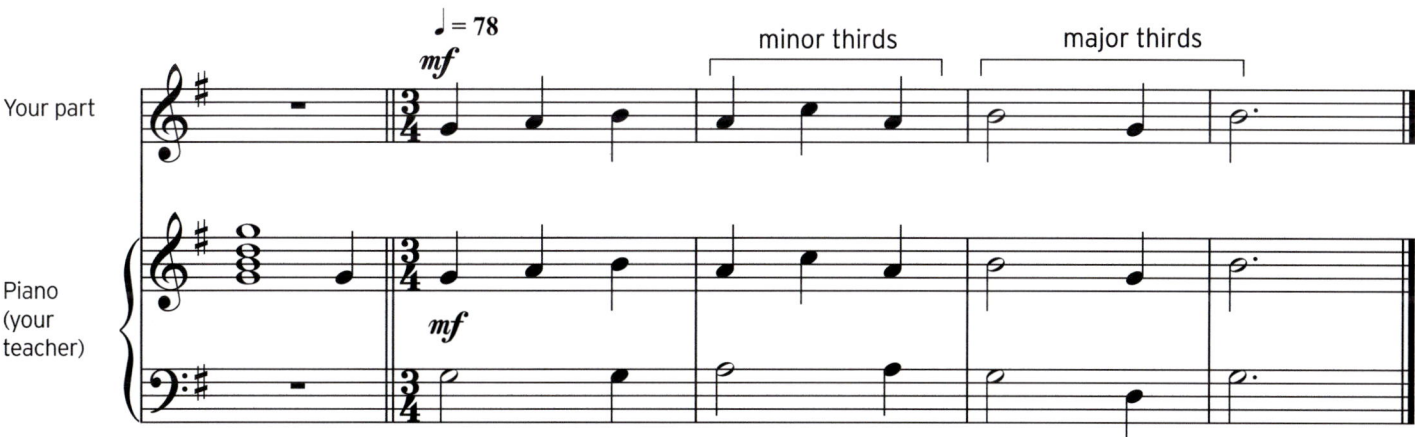

59

Grade 2

Lesson 4

- **Practise reading in the time signature 4/4**
- **Practise reading semibreves**
- **Major thirds in different keys**

4/4 means four crotchets in a bar. The upper 4 shows how many beats and the lower 4 indicates the kind of beat (in this case – crotchets)

o **semibreve**. A semibreve lasts for four crotchet beats.

In G major we know there is a major third between G and B, but in C major there is a major third between C and E, and in F major between F and A. Circle all the major thirds that you can find, then have a go at singing these exercises.

1

2

3

4

5

Grade 2

Think before you sing:

Identify the time signature – how many beats per bar?

Identify the key signature – is this phrase written in C major, G major or F major?

Look ahead to see where the tricky sections are so that you are prepared.

Accompanied Exercise

Grade 2

Lesson 5

- Different keys and time signatures

This time, see if you can read a little bit ahead while you are singing. You will be amazed at how much your brain can absorb in advance.

Before you start each exercise, check the key and time signature and have a look through to observe any awkward moments.

Tap the rhythm first, then hum the tonic (key note) and go from there.

Grade 2

Think before you sing:

Have you identified the time signature?

Do you know which key the exercise is written in?

Have you identified any tricky areas in the exercise?

Accompanied Exercise

Here you will sing a major third, but the first bar prepares you for it by just going up a major second first.

Grade 2

Lesson 6

- **The dynamic *mp***

mp sign is an abbreviation of *mezzo-piano*. *Piano* means 'soft' and *mezzo* means 'half' or 'fairly', so we interpret *mp* as being moderately soft.

Before you start each exercise, have a look through and observe any awkward moments and make sure you notice if the dynamic is *mf* or *mp*.

In exercise 3, make sure that you count the full three beats on the first note.

Grade 2

Think before you sing:

Have you identified the time signature?

Do you know which key the exercise is written in?

What dynamic is it?

Accompanied Exercise

Grade 2

Lesson 7

- Reading ahead

There are just a few more awkward moments this time. Read ahead and you will be prepared for them.

Draw a bracket under all the thirds in these exercises – there are 15 to find!

Grade 2

Think before you sing:

Have you identified the time signature?

Do you know which key the exercise is written in?

What dynamic is it?

Accompanied Exercise

Tap the rhythm, hum the key note and off you go, trying to read ahead.

67

Lesson 8

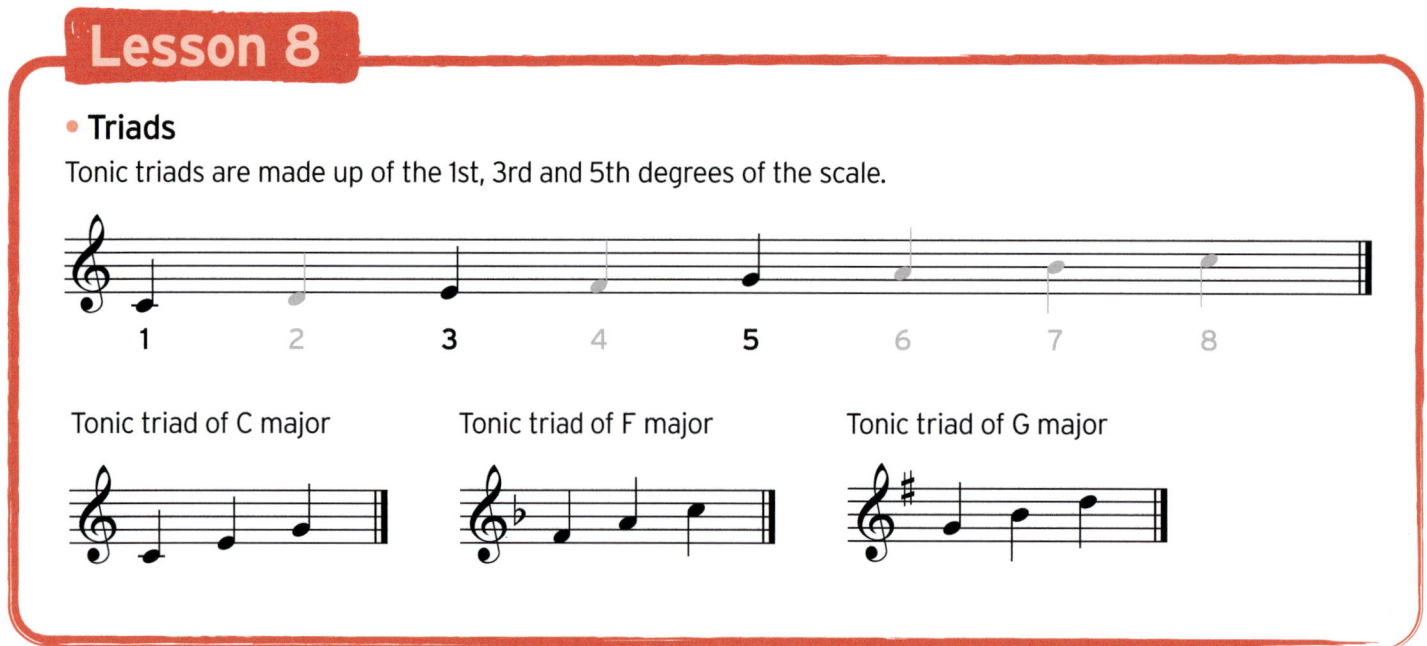

Triads

Tonic triads are made up of the 1st, 3rd and 5th degrees of the scale.

Tonic triad of C major

Tonic triad of F major

Tonic triad of G major

Spot the tonic triads in these exercises, then try to sing them.

1

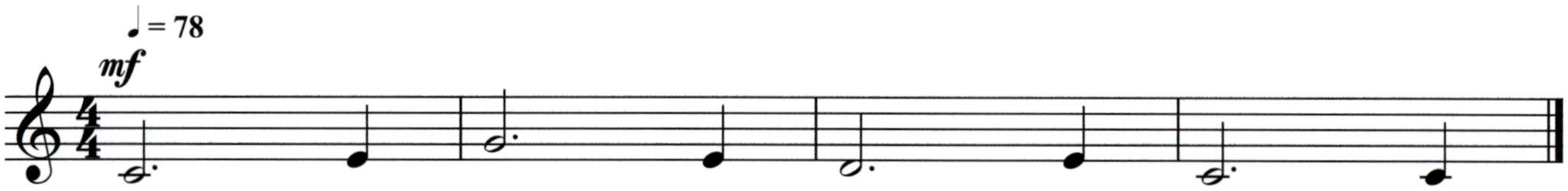

2

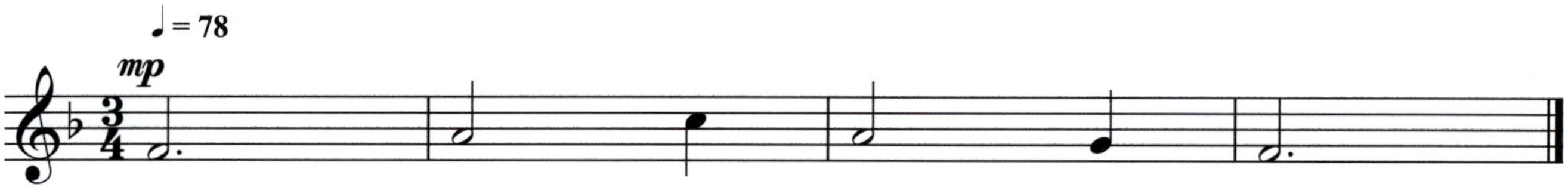

3

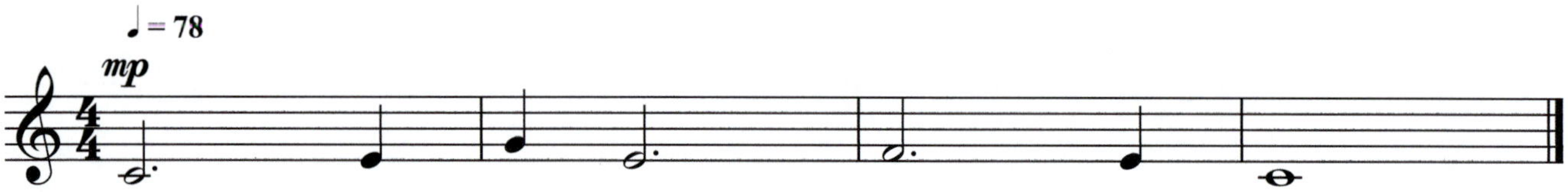

4

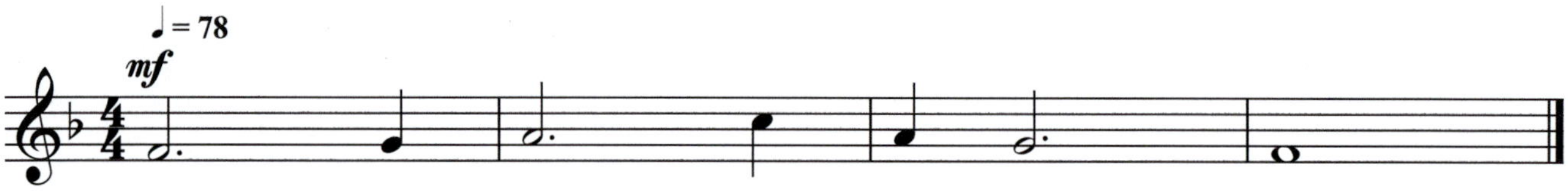

5

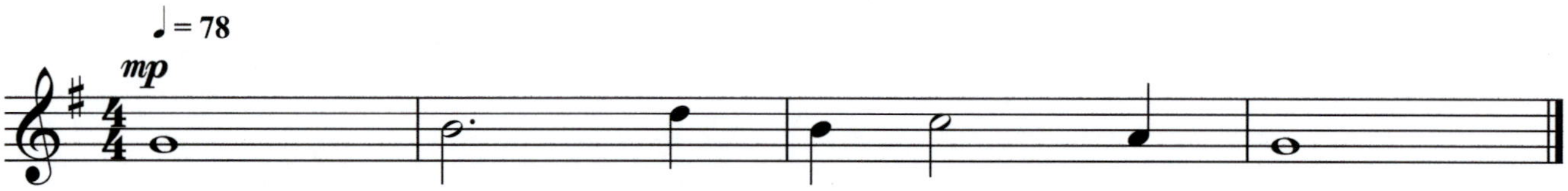

Grade 2

Think before you sing:

Have you identified the time signature?

Do you know which key the exercise is written in?

Can you spot a triad in that key?

Accompanied Exercise

Grade 2

Lesson 9

- **More work with triads**

Spot the triads before you sing. There are some unexpected turns here, so read ahead.

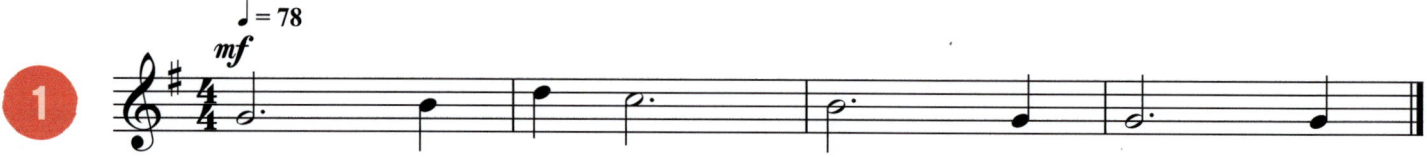

Grade 2

Think before you sing:

Have you identified the time signature and dynamic?

Do you know which key the exercise is written in?

Spot the dynamic marking

Accompanied Exercise

Grade 2

Lesson 10

- **Keeping hold of the key note (tonic)**

Make sure that you keep hearing the key note throughout each exercise. Even if the key note does not return in the exercise, this is still useful to do, as you can relate each note that you are singing back to the key note.

Eg, in exercise 3, the final note is an A, which is a major third above the key note. If you have the F in your mind, you can imagine the F tonic triad, which should help in pitching that final note.

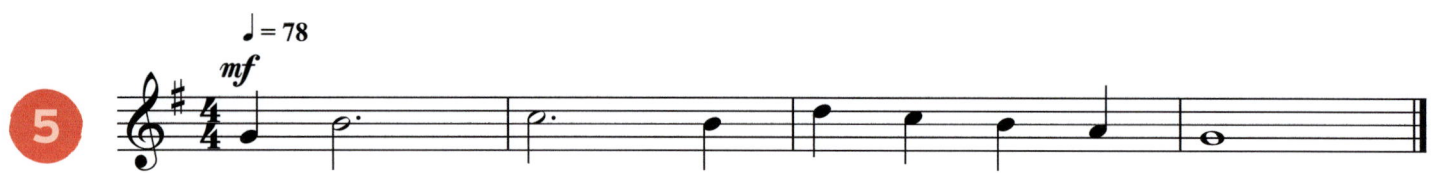

Grade 2

Think before you sing:

Have you identified the time signature and dynamic?

Do you know which key the exercise is written in?

Have you identified any tricky areas in the exercise?

Accompanied Exercise

There are several thirds, major and minor here. If in doubt, hear the two seconds that make up each of them.

Grade 2

Specimen Sight Reading Tests

Remember to use all of the ideas and techniques from the previous lessons when approaching sight reading.

1a. Interval Test
Please sing this note, and a major third above it. **[Play the lower note of the two printed]**

1b. Rhythm Test
Please clap the rhythm of this line straight through. **[Clap the pulse while counting 2 bars aloud]**

1c. Sung Test
You have 30 seconds to prepare for the sung part of the test, during which time you may practise aloud. You can choose which sound you use for this part of the test (dee/da/la).
[Play the key chord and starting note before and after the 30 seconds. Count 2 bars aloud.]

Grade 2

2a. Interval Test

2b. Rhythm Test

2c. Sung Test

3a. Interval Test

3b. Rhythm Test

3c. Sung Test

Grade 2

4a. Interval Test

4b. Rhythm Test

4c. Sung Test

5a. Interval Test

5b. Rhythm Test

5c. Sung Test

Grade 2

6a. Interval Test

6b. Rhythm Test

6c. Sung Test

7a. Interval Test

7b. Rhythm Test

7c. Sung Test

Grade 2

8a. Interval Test

8b. Rhythm Test

8c. Sung Test

9a. Interval Test

9b. Rhythm Test

9c. Sung Test

10a. Interval Test

10b. Rhythm Test

10c. Sung Test